THE UNOFFICIAL GUIDE TO
CONFLICT RESOLUTION IN MINECRAFT

JILL KEPPELER

PowerKiDS press

Published in 2026 by The Rosen Publishing Group, Inc.
2544 Clinton Street, Buffalo, NY 14224

Copyright © 2026 by The Rosen Publishing Group, Inc.

All rights reserved. No part of this book may be reproduced in any form without permission in writing from the publisher, except by a reviewer.

First Edition

Editor: Greg Roza
Book Design: Rachel Rising
Illustrator: Matías Lapegüe

Photo Credits: Cover, p. 1 Soloma/Shutterstock.com; Cover, pp. 1, 3, 4, 6, 9, 11, 13 14, 16, 18, 20–24 Oksana Kalashnykova/Shutterstock.com; Cover, pp. 1, 4, 6, 8–13, 14, 16, 18, 19, 20, 22–24 SkillUp/Shutterstock.com; Cover, pp. 1, 3, 4, 6, 9, 11, 13, 14, 16, 18, 20, 22–24 gersamina donnichi/Shutterstock.com; p. 15 Krakenimages.com/Shutterstock.com.

Library of Congress Cataloging-in-Publication Data

Names: Keppeler, Jill, author.
Title: The unofficial guide to conflict resolution in Minecraft / Jill
   Keppeler.
Description: [Buffalo] : PowerKids Press, [2026] | Series: The unofficial
   guide to Minecraft social skills | Includes index. | Audience term:
   Children
Identifiers: LCCN 2025006096 (print) | LCCN 2025006097 (ebook) | ISBN
   9781499452853 (library binding) | ISBN 9781499452846 (paperback) | ISBN
   9781499452860 (ebook)
Subjects: LCSH: Conflict management–Juvenile literature. | Minecraft
   (Game)–Juvenile literature.
Classification: LCC HM1126 .K47 2026 (print) | LCC HM1126 (ebook) | DDC
   794.8/5-dc23/eng/20250213
LC record available at https://lccn.loc.gov/2025006096
LC ebook record available at https://lccn.loc.gov/2025006097

Manufactured in the United States of America

Some of the images in this book illustrate individuals who are models. The depictions do not imply actual situations or events.

CPSIA Compliance Information: Batch #CSPK26. For Further Information contact Rosen Publishing at 1-800-237-9932.

CONTENTS

SHARING A WORLD 4

SETTING RULES 6

CAUSES OF CONFLICT 8

RECOGNIZING PROBLEMS 10

UNDERSTANDING FEELINGS 12

COMMUNICATE! 14

COMING TO BLOWS 16

CONSEQUENCES 18

MOVING FORWARD 20

GLOSSARY 22

FOR MORE INFORMATION 23

INDEX 24

SHARING A WORLD

The sandbox game *Minecraft* can be many things. You can play in a world with unlimited **resources** in which you can fly and build whatever you want. You can play in a peaceful world to explore or a world with many monsters to battle. And you can play alone—or you can play with friends in the same world!

While it can be a lot of fun to play with others, it also means that you can have different issues. People can disagree and want to play in different ways. That's OK, but what happens when this leads to conflict? If you want to keep playing together, you'll have to figure it out.

MINECRAFT MANIA

A *Minecraft* world in creative **mode** means you can't get hurt, have unlimited resources and can fly. In a survival world, though, you can get hurt and need to eat.

Every player in a *Minecraft* world can create their own "skin," or the appearance of their character.

SETTING RULES

When playing in a new *Minecraft* world with other people, it can be good to start out with basic rules. Is the world going to be focused on building? Exploring? **Combat**? If the combat is with other players, everyone should know starting out. Is taking resources from other players part of your game? What about damaging, or hurting, their buildings?

It's important to know that when *Minecraft* players are in a shared world, that world may be "owned" by one of them. If so, that person may need and want a bigger say in the rules.

MINECRAFT MANIA

A *Minecraft* Realm is a **server** on which you can play with your friends. One of those friends (or likely a parent or other adult) will be the owner. They will need to invite people to play.

Building in *Minecraft* can be a lot of fun. Different materials have different strengths and weaknesses. For example, wood can burn!

CAUSES OF CONFLICT

With rules, communication is important. Everyone should know them. Conflict will start when people don't! Of course, it can also start when some people know but don't follow the rules. This can be especially **frustrating**. What if you've all agreed that stealing isn't allowed, but one player keeps going into other people's bases and taking their stuff?

Also, sometimes what seems to be the cause of a conflict isn't so simple. Maybe one player is upset because another player teamed up with someone else. They may say (and even think) they're upset because it's unfair because the team has too many resources. But really, maybe it's because they thought that other player was their friend and should team up with them.

MINECRAFT MANIA

Why would a *Minecraft* world ever allow stealing? Well, it can be fun to create things to protect your stuff! You can make traps for other players, **security** systems for your base, and other fun builds.

You can make a basic *Minecraft* chest to put your stuff in with eight wooden planks. There's also a way to turn a chest into a trapped chest to protect it!

9

RECOGNIZING PROBLEMS

So, how do you recognize the problems that can lead to conflict? The simple answer is just to pay attention to your friends. Listening actively is important. And if you see something you think is unfair, other people probably think it's unfair too. What if you've spent a lot of time and emeralds building up village traders, but someone else comes in and uses up all the best trades? You'd be upset!

Empathy is important to this. Imagine how others feel. If you do, maybe you can stop those problems before they become full conflicts that cause lots of bad feelings.

MINECRAFT MANIA

Villagers in *Minecraft* start as novices. There are five levels. As you trade with them, they become apprentices, journeymen, experts, and finally, masters. Masters have the best trades.

Trading with villagers can be a great way to get different resources in *Minecraft*. Farmer villagers like these often will trade crops.

UNDERSTANDING FEELINGS

Sometimes, of course, you'll be the one having these feelings. You could be sad or mad if friends team up in the *Minecraft* world and leave you out. You could be upset or frustrated if someone else finds a resource you've been searching for (like a village or a pale garden **biome**) and won't share. You might want to do or say something to show how upset you are.

Sometimes it's good to share your feelings. Sometimes, though, you need to remember that you can't take some things back. If you call people names or damage someone's base, people might not want to play with you again.

MINECRAFT MANIA

 Pale garden biomes in *Minecraft* are newer biomes and have lots of unique, or one-of-a-kind, resources. There are pale oak trees, creaking mobs, and **resin** clumps.

Pale gardens got their name because they don't have much color. They can be hard to find!

COMMUNICATE!

Once you've recognized your feelings or the feelings of others that might be causing conflict, you can work on dealing with them. Identify both those feelings and what's causing them. Talk to the people involved in a conflict. What do they want to see happen? Maybe some rules need to be changed. Maybe they need to be explained better.

Either way, it's important there be some communication and agreement. While one player may be a leader in the world, making rules for everyone without communication is a good way to lose all the people you wanted to play with. That's no fun!

MINECRAFT MANIA

Griefing in *Minecraft* and other online games means harassing or annoying other players just for fun, not as part of any attempt to play the game. It can cause lots of problems.

COMING TO BLOWS

Even if you use these ways to manage conflict in your *Minecraft* world, sometimes it won't be enough. Feelings can get the better of people, and when they do, these feelings can explode into big problems. People might let these feelings out in ways that damage, or hurt, what others have built. They can even hurt or kill other players if you have a survival world.

When this happens, it might first be best to take a break. Let people cool down before things get worse. It can be much harder to resolve a conflict when you're still very angry and hurt.

MINECRAFT MANIA

Your gameplay might include battles or combat between players. But this is very different from having a fellow player attack you unexpectedly. A player might not have weapons or armor if they're not expecting to fight.

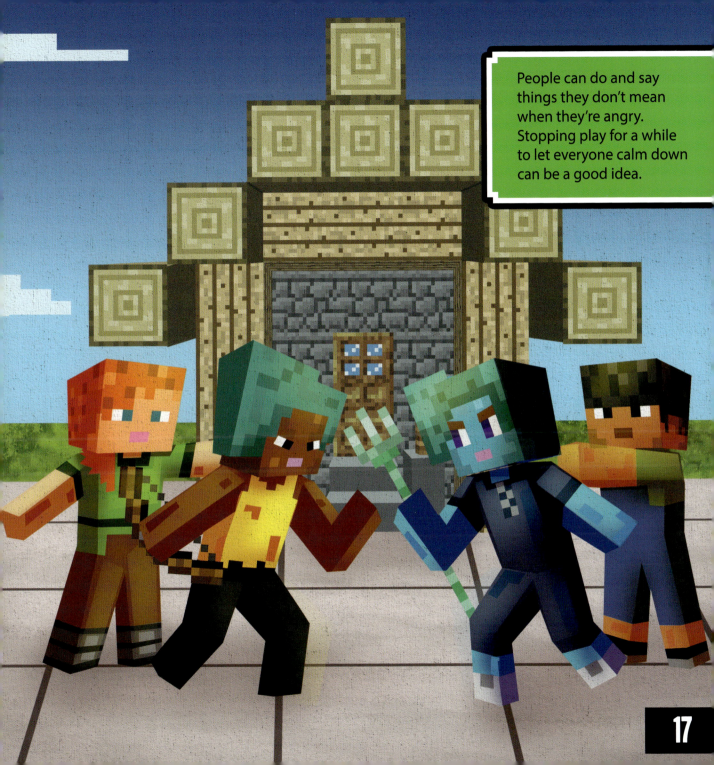

CONSEQUENCES

Once people have calmed down, players need to talk about the conflict and how to move forward. Maybe just a warning will work for small problems, but sometimes players may need to see some real change before they want to play again. Maybe a problem player needs **consequences** for their actions. Or maybe they just need to **apologize**. Maybe both!

For example, if one player causes conflict by taking other players' diamonds, perhaps all the other players could agree that player needs to pay those diamonds back, maybe with some extras. Just remember that any rules should apply to everyone.

MINECRAFT MANIA

Diamonds are one of the rarer resources in *Minecraft*. They can be used to make some of the best tools and weapons in the game.

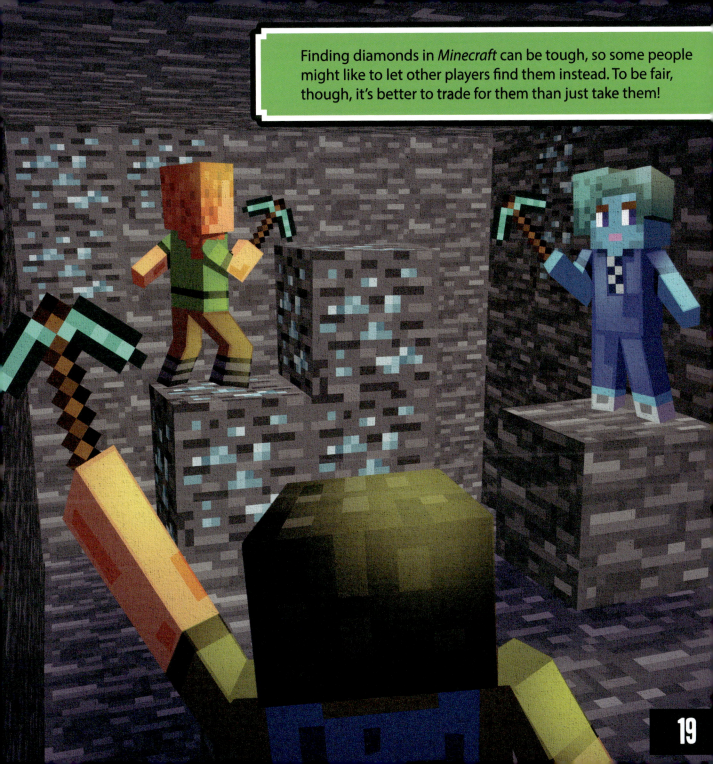

Finding diamonds in *Minecraft* can be tough, so some people might like to let other players find them instead. To be fair, though, it's better to trade for them than just take them!

MOVING FORWARD

Sometimes it can be hard to know the right way to resolve a conflict. What other players might agree is a good idea (like making another player pay back stolen diamonds) won't always work. What's important is to try and to be willing to go on to a new plan if needed.

You and your friends could come up with a list of ideas and write them down. If you need to, you could go to a trusted adult for help practicing tough conversations, or talks. With practice, you and your friends can learn how to deal with conflict…and keep the conflict to fighting zombies!

MINECRAFT MANIA

Having a team and working together can make some *Minecraft* problems easier. When a group of zombies is attacking you, it's great to have friends to come to your rescue!

Teamwork makes it easier to beat *Minecraft's* many monsters!

GLOSSARY

apologize: To say that you're sorry for something you've done.

biome: A natural community of plants and animals, such as a forest or desert.

combat: A fight or contest.

consequence: Something that is a result of something else.

empathy: Understanding or being aware of and feeling the emotions of others.

frustrating: Having to do with an act that makes someone feel discouraged.

mode: A version, or form of something that is different from others.

resin: A partly clear substance produced by trees.

resource: Something that can be used.

security: Something meant to keep something safe.

server: A computer in a network that provides services or files to others.

FOR MORE INFORMATION

BOOKS

Levy, Adir, and Ganit Levy. *What Should Darla Do? Featuring the Power to Choose*. Miami, FL: Elon Books, 2020.

Mojang AB. *Minecraft: Guide to Survival*. New York, NY: Random House Worlds, 2022.

Reed, Josh. *Conflict Resolution for Kids*. Josh Reed, 2024.

WEBSITES

Trading
minecraft.wiki/w/Trading
Learn more about trading with villagers.

What's the Best Way to Resolve Conflict?
wonderopolis.org/wonder/What's-the-Best-Way-To-Resolve-Conflict
Wonderopolis offers advice on confliction resolution for kids.

Publisher's note to educators and parents: Our editors have carefully reviewed these websites to ensure that they are suitable for students. Many websites change frequently, however, and we cannot guarantee that a site's future contents will continue to meet our high standards of quality and educational value. Be advised that students should be closely supervised whenever they access the internet.

INDEX

C

communication, 8, 14
consequences, 18

E

empathy, 10

F

feelings, 10, 12, 14

G

griefing, 14, 15

L

listening, 10

R

Realms, 6
rules, 6, 8, 14, 16, 18

S

server, 6
share, 6, 12
stealing, 8, 9

T

take a break, 16, 17
teamwork, 20, 21
trades, 10, 11, 19